# Firstborn

Books by Franco Pagnucci

*Breath of the Onion: Italian-American Anecdotes* (North Star Press, 2015)

*Tracks on Damp Sand* (North Star Press, 2014)

*All That Is Left* (Chapbook, Red Ochre Lit, 2012)

*Ancient Moves* (Bur Oak Press, 1998)

*I Never Had a Pet* (Bur Oak Press, 1992)

*Out Harmsen's Way* (Fireweed Press, 1991)


Anthologies Edited by Franco Pagnucci

*New Roads Old Towns* (A Rountree Publication, University of Wisconsin–Platteville, 1988)

*Face the Poem* (Bur Oak Press, 1979)

# Firstborn

Franco Pagnucci

NORTH STAR PRESS OF ST. CLOUD, INC.
St. Cloud, Minnesota

*for Susan*
*who is a gift*

ISBN: 978-1-68201-024-2

Printed in the United States of America.

First edition: March 2016

Published by:
North Star Press of St. Cloud, Inc.
P.O. Box 451
St. Cloud, MN 56302

www.northstarpress.com

# Contents

## 1
## An Ending

## 2
## Firstborn

3

A Resurrection

# 1
# An Ending

## This Pair of Eagles

This pair of bald eagles make pretty good neighbors. They are mostly around and keep close to their place. Often he sits on the top branch of the white pine, and she ten feet below, on the huge stick nest, at the center of the tree. They call to each other, coming and going, and you might see and hear the flapping like a great kite catching wind as they lift off or come in, but they are hardly wild or aggressive. Huge birds that they are, they seem as evenly disposed as your largest of people—serious, family oriented, and, in a way, down to earth. Not like crows and ravens that are always cawing and making a ruckus.

Let a passing crow or raven spot or hear one of these eagles . . .

Crows and ravens are merciless. They'll dive an eagle from above and behind, screaming caws and pecking at them, trying to yank out a tail feather.

Crows and ravens unsettle these eagles. They make them flinch and crane their necks and make them twist their heads like owls. They make them whine like loons.

## How Many Times

have we missed
the unfurled
soft tips of the ferns?
How many times have you opened a palm,
and I missed the gesture
or misread the intent?

Later, I'm here
or in some other room,
and you, too, are on your own
so that we have to stop to find each other,
to say again, "Here I am." The other says, "Yes,"
eyes unblinking, wide as open arms.

# Dear Ralph

—for Ralph Comstock, groundskeeper,
wildflower preserve (1883?–1969)

Half a lifetime since you showed me how to look, and I've planted trees everywhere I've lived: birch and maple, apple and pear, spruce and red pine, white pine and red and white cedar, water willow and pin oak, sour cherries and peach trees that made a *festa* of fruit one early summer and early fall. Even the Chinese chestnuts, a strain immune to the old blight, gave us sweet nuts to roast a late October. *Papà's* fig tree had to be buried in November and resurrected in April, but there were sweet, black Mission Figs in some late Septembers in northern Illinois.

If you could awaken like a new maple shoot, and why not, you could come down our long, tree-lined drive, proud to know us as any friend. The spruce and red pine and maple stand waiting, waiting tall every day for you to walk toward the house.

# Ron's World

Dusk darkened the windows,
the room disappearing
into the mahogany wall-bookcase along one wall
and, along the other,
a closed, black-walnut floor-to-ceiling TV cabinet and black-
  hearth fireplace.
In between, Ron was all but gone.

Only the sound of his shaking right shoulder, arm and hand,
faintly outlined his diminished frame
that couldn't control the Parkinson's trembling
even with the left hand clamped over the right.
The wound-taut spring ticked and ticked
the eternal clock out of his control,
his word or two trailing off as hoarse whispers in need of air,
air and saliva—water, probably.

Suddenly rising,
"Don't mind me," he'd say.
"You just keep on . . . .
I need to stand and move a bit
to keep myself in place."

# The Wind and the Green

In the morning
the wind
fluttered a thousand leaves
and spread the chirps
and twitters of unseen
birds. The green

was a comfort, too,
slipping by the curtains
coming in,
and that light
touched the darkest corners,
gave your urge a lift.

# The Happiest Days

—for *Mamma* (1912–2008)

These are the happiest days of mothering for her, I want to imagine. What with the housekeeping a few minutes' chore and with only one fledgling to care for. Early spring has made fish plentiful, now, and easy, even if her eaglet is ravenous, growing in leaps, feathers already coming in between the downy fuzz. With the warm spring and the eaglet warm enough, she is free to wander off for a few turns over the lake to fish each afternoon. Though *Mamma*, herself, would have never done it, she would sympathize with that need.

After the mother eagle comes back and they've shared the fish she brought and she has cleaned the mess from under her young and has waggled herself back against the snoozing, that's when she is most comforted, knowing her young is safest, then, and within the circle of her domain.

## I See Her Fussing

I see her standing on the edge and fussing over the nest, and you can hear little peeps, whines, and groans, as if the young one hates to be bothered or to be moved and would rather lie in the mess.

When the male eagle flops down onto the opposite edge of the great stick nest, then you recognize the flurry of squawks, the complaints for his benefit, really, though the male eagle knows not to interfere and he hops up to his usual lookout branch.

Then, she preens the eaglet's matted fuzz, lifting and turning new dark feathers, making the eaglet stretch the neck upward with the tickle that's almost enjoyable and blink the huge eyes that seem too big for that head.

It's a rainy morning, besides, with a cold nip to the wind, so the eaglet is glad when *Mamma* quits fussing and waggles down with her feathery warmth and calm, thumping chest.

## Three Young Geese

They plucked the first seed heads off dandelions.
Two adult geese followed with soft chortles guarding

and guiding. The young had come up the path
from the lake and found a green, open patch for a picnic.

Thoughts made a field of daisies swaying in the wind
though it was still April. Foxy snow would often slink in.

## Complaint

Sometimes her whistles turn to whines when he's been gone too long. It's the usual complaint, you understand. She's got to be there. It gets long . . . all day . . . Everyday the same. And all night. When she hops up to a branch to cool her shoulders and backside, to untangle the taut springs of her wings and to loosen the knots that have crept up her legs, still, she can't take her eyes off the eaglet. Not for a moment. So many crows and ravens hang out nearby, now. She'd like to soar a turn or two and skim over the lake, while the fish are moving. She'd like to search far and wide and along the warm, shallow shore she hardly remembers.

## Dear *Mamma*

This child . . .
I wish you'd known her . . .
How she'll run to meet your arrival,
light-blue Crocs splaying, feet flying.
How she'll fill a room and an out-of-doors with cartwheels
to the left, to the right, bits of word-songs spinning in the air.
How she'll say, "You know what . . . ?" and "You know what . . . ?"
her face a wide, morning sky.

If you were here, I would say, *You know what, Mamma?*
*This child is her mother . . . Oh, her mother,*
*who once, after a walk, had us walk back*
*to the place where she had picked up*
*a bird's yellow tail feather.*
*We had to return that feather*
*in case the bird came back looking for it.*

*And you know what?*
*This, this child has curls*
*and eyes . . . Yes,*
*she has the cat eyes . . .*
*the intense-blue cat eyes*
*you disparaged*
*of the woman I married.*
*Yes. Oh yes.*

## Cerulean Warbler

There were some black streaks, too,
and two white wing bars
and the white underparts,
but the blue-gray of the back,
blued in your eyes as he moved in
and out of the underbrush along shore.

It was a short wave
of a small light from across the lake
or the blue pulse of a star while you stare.
It was like that first open-arm kiss in a March wind
you keep trying to remember.

## As They Flew

As they flew,
their caws barked and crackled
behind them above the trees.

Suddenly the two lifted their heads and wings upward
and went at each other, clawing like eagles.

Maybe violence
unleashed changes the face of even two ordinary crows.
Looking up, that's what we saw.

## May 13, 2012

Though they hadn't slept together
for ten years (as she had told us once)
she said that night he had come to her room before midnight
and that they lay side by side in her bed talking
most of the night.

            Once their shoulders
or a foot touched, and she felt a tingling
spiral down her left side and felt her thighs
get warm. The back of her neck, her shoulders
got hot and damp downward to the small of her back.

Even months after, the thought made warm-shivers
run along her spine, and she wished she had thought
to tell him, *Later, talk won't be enough. Not nearly.*
But they had long forgotten that way of talking.
Not saying anything was a way not to feel bad or be at fault.
*He never said a thing. Why should she?*
Talking would only lead to bickering was her thought.
And anyway, nothing she could have said would
have made a difference. His mind was made up.
He'd been searching on the Internet for ways
for two years. Not one to decide anything
spur of the moment, he explored the angles.
All the pros and cons.

That night he told her, "The kids will
have a good Memorial Day without me.
It's got to be now, before the shaking gets
so as it'll be impossible to do
or I'm a drooling, twisted mess."

She said he worried about burning up the kid's
inheritance. "I agreed," she told us. "What with costs
of medicines and care these days. He was thinking
practical to the end." She said to us,
"I have to thank him for that."
She said, "I really do."

I could have chimed in on the *thoughtful*
and the *practical*. When I visited and we'd be talking
into late afternoon, he would turn on the dimmest lamp,
the one with the birch-wood shade he'd turned out of a chunk
of a trunk his son-in-law had cut. As we talked, sometimes
the room would be so dark, but for his shaking side and arm,
I wouldn't know if he was even there.

## We Go Out Early

In a warmer morning,
in a world alive with birds
and the grosbeak's notes
cascading on the wind,
I wished I had thought
to tell him, *We need you here
to listen to the birds.*

## Crow in the Rain

Heavy rains blinded the tree-lined road
one side to the other, at times
casting a gray wall even over the treetops.
The low sky disappeared, and the small
crow along the left shoulder stood
wet-backed and alone.

                             Having come late,
maybe she hung too long over the blood
splotch on the road, trying to make amends,
while heavy rains gathered. Now unable to leave,
maybe a little lost, you could see how drowned
feathers smudged her glossy black back.
You could feel her downcast stance.

## Ahead of Us

A fluttering of dragonflies
over the gravel road.

Some veered off under trees,
and more and more rose,
as the morning sun caught their amber wings,
a dusting of silver on copper.

And they kept rising and rising ahead of us,
so you knew they could lift us, too,
above the cool and the damp
if we let them.

# 2
# Firstborn

## On Your Birthday, June 12, 2010

—for Gian (1967–   )

Morning. A gray day of heavy clouds and dark. Really dark. Rain expected, fog, mist—all day. And we were headed out . . .

But there it was on the edge of the stick nest. Standing!

Early June, and it was huge already. The black feathers coming in spiky all over like a lead singer's head or as if they were wet and needed combing on this frizzy hair day. The eaglet stood there, on the edge of the nest, at that great height for us to see it—dark as the day, beautiful as the lush and wet green of that early June, against the dark.

After a time, maybe after we'd been satisfied enough, it peeped once, then settled back down into the nest and out of sight.

## By the Library Doors

The branches of the Juneberry bush bent
and bounced in the wind and enfolded each other
like leafy strands of hair.

A gust brought waxwings, an armful of black-tufted,
soft olive-colored birds—thoughts on a mouthful of air.

Those birds came and worked on the berries,
the branches swaying in wind like a field of ripe barley,
the workers heading home happy with bundles on their shoulders.

## A Question of the Sandhill Cranes

We heard them. You could look out over the rows of corn that weren't as tall yet as a standing crane, but even when one of us walked across the gravel path that ended at the cornfield's edge and stood glancing down into the deep gully that had a little run-off water . . .

We had to go on with only the guttural chatter of cranes. No sightings. And then the chatter ended, and each of us had to re-imagine cranes we'd seen in other places—their rust-colored feathers, their definitive stance, surprising as exclamations or question marks in a green field along County M.

## Snapping Turtles

They came early.
To protect the holes where they buried their eggs,
I raked their trails and scrapes

off the gravel drive.
When we go out, maybe it's good to remember
we might be walking on eggs.

# The Goose

You could tell it wasn't her first time, the way the goose neck
draped itself like a limp snake into the grassy hummock nest.
The bill almost parted and the gray chin, slightly tilted, could
suggest the impact when she dropped from flight.

All, all got your sympathy.

And you had to applaud the authentic scene in spite of the
few fringes of white down fluff that crept from under her belly.
There was a mastery of bird and bush and art.

## A Black Bear Looked at Us

A large black bear
crossed the road,
climbed the steep bank
on the right, and stopped
and turned his head
to look at us.

So you had to notice
the deep, glossy, bluish-blackness
and the great size
and the wildness rippling
off his shoulders and sides—
a mysterious blessed wildness.

## Severe Storm

### 1.

In the night we didn't know. You could hear the wind gather and rush. It stopped at the northwest end the lake for an instant and sat on its haunches, shoulders and arms thrown back . . . then it hurtled itself, an avalanche of spray over the house and with a brush of hard bristles scattered branches and ripped and shredded leaves. The rain came—sheets and buckets hurled at us. Then the spray. And a breather, before it all started again with the wind.

### 2.

All morning it was dim with a heavy damp, but when the clouds scattered, the sky opened blue with a hot light, a hot light we remembered from other years, and it was all right.

## Saturday

### 1. Morning

We found the immature bald eagle on a low stump, up the hill of the gravel road that dead ends at our drive. It was mid-morning, the July day already hazy and steamy.

She would have come down after a hesitant step off the edge of the stick nest in the top of the white pine and would have fallen into a downhill glide too sudden and reached the ground too fast and with a thump. She would have thumped her large chest like a top-heavy turkey, this piper of primitive notes. She would have thumped the ground in a heap, on forgotten claws stuck out like an armful of kindling.

Surprised at the closeness of earth, the hardness of the leafy moss on the grassy knoll, harder than the stick nest she'd left up there, her eyes followed us and followed the wide, soft-stepping arc we made past her stump-stand and then back.

She knew us and had watched our anxious concern for months as she stood on the edge of the stick nest and looked down, often thinking of leaping out. Now there was no going back. She was here among us, unafraid, and we were here.

## 2. Evening

The eaglet stood mid-point on the trunk of the wind-dropped oak that sat on its three-foot stump and leaned out toward the river channel.

I didn't say it, but I was happy to see her as our canoe rounded the southeast lip of land on Robinson Lake. The river flowed lazily for a quarter-mile and was sheltered from wind before it entered a shallow but 200-acre Birch Lake. I was glad she had moved off the stump on the knoll above the road, a vulnerable place, where she'd spent her day after leaving the nest. "At least she's facing water," I said. "She doesn't know water and needs to learn where fish live."

"Eagles have good eyes," you said. "Great eyes. When we got married, we went off on our own, so you could go on to school. I didn't know anything. How to do anything. Being far from family, I had no one to watch. No one to ask."

"Some things . . . you knew some things," I said with a half-smile, though you couldn't see my face since I sat in front and you sat in the stern of the canoe, as usual.

"You might be surprised," you said. "Even about that."

One of the immature's parents left the tall white pine and glided over the river channel and went on across Robinson Lake behind us where the sun had set. Strands of orange glow coming through the trees on our right lit the swarms of bugs ahead of us toward Birch Lake. We went on in our own silence, content as the canoe.

# Sunday Morning, July 11

As we came around our southeast point of land and into the
river channel to Birch Lake, the eaglet was still on the same
wind-dropped oak trunk that leaned from its stump, two to
three feet above the ground. She had moved closer to the water
now, and as our canoe floated us past, I saw her large, large yel-
low claws. Like a child with big feet, I thought, she'll grow to
fill big shoes. Large shoes for a girl. And her bill so black, so
huge, seemed too large for her head.

But she had made it safely through the night, in spite of the
red fox who stalks that point, the coyote who makes occasional
rounds, and the lone wolf who visits once or twice a year.

I was happy for her that Sunday morning, though her pink
tongue hung out between the parted bill in the airless morning
and already too-heavy day. The heat of the day before was
awake early and reaching up. The lake was drawing itself in
tighter and receding deeper, preserving its wetness after a dry
June.

If it proved a hot, dry July, it would not be the best of sum-
mers to learn all this bird had to learn. Already, she seemed too
big, this eaglet, who had stayed in the nest too long. She seemed
too heavy to get the proper lift, the lift she needed for her wings
to raise her above the treetops where she might catch the winds
that soar.

# Spread-Eagled

Monday morning the immature eagle was in Rose's bottom, peeping and peeping, as usual, the thin squeals, and all day we heard her but didn't see her.

Next morning she was on Rose's cabin roof, spread-eagled, on the eastern side in the sun. Lying on her back as she was with wings fanned out, I thought that she had crashed there like a dumb, too-heavy chicken trying to fly. I thought my story ended before I'd begun to consider how she might adjust, finally, after fledging late and leaving the nest reluctantly, her parents unpracticed in family ways and unsure, and the world harsh as always and all the harsher for any off-center responder.

For sure, it seemed a sad ending, except that when I turned and walked back up the hill and toward Schiess Road, I saw her head of unkempt, dry feathers rise over the roof ridge and her right eye look at me, and I know a breath leaped from under my ribs, up and over my dry lips.

# In the Afternoon

In the late afternoon of her fourth day out in the world, as I walked toward the back of the house, searching for the immature bald eagle, I saw her come gliding toward a young maple downhill below the side of the garage, and I saw her try to land on a small branch of that tree, about thirty feet off the ground. She missed the branch and fell as if she'd been shot. I heard the loud clunk of her chest against the tree trunk, and I saw her drop three or four feet, bark pieces and crumbles of bark and bark dust falling, as she dropped, before one of her claws snagged a knob of bark and trunk and she bounced another hard thud against the trunk and stopped and held suspended. Her wings were stretched below her hanging head like a climber who'd slipped and tumbled backwards and now hung by a foot from her rope, head down toward the depths.

She began to flap and thunk her wings upward against the trunk then, trying to right herself. More bark dust and pieces of bark flew up around her and fell, and I felt my face grow hot and redden, and I shifted uncomfortably as I watched, remembering when they picked me, the new foreign kid in St. Pat's third grade, for center field. I remembered the fly ball that came right to me. I saw the big ball and felt it hit and watched it drop from my unpracticed, reaching hands.

When she finally let go and dropped and slid into a downhill glide, she saw and landed on a wind-felled popple, wobbly at first, but she straightened herself, her ruffled outfit. One loose feather blew in a warm waft of ground wind as she raised and held her speckled head and huge black bill in a patriotic pose.

# Five Days Into the World

We heard the bald eaglet calling in the gray morning and looked out our bedroom window and saw her on the peak of the garage.

After a while we watched her open her wings and fly up onto the steep peak of the house. You could see the effort it took her to get enough lift for the extra half-dozen feet of elevation. For hours she stayed on the roof ridge of the house. Now and then we heard her heavy clopping, one end to the other, like a toddler in her first hard-soled shoes.

When I went out looking up, she leaned her head over the edge of the peak to look down at me. Each time I aimed the camera, she leaned down the side of her head closest to me, to look with her right eye or left. You might have thought we were playing peek-a-boo.

As the heavy rains came, she was still on the house peak. Now and then, we could hear her heavy-stepping. We went out, then, and stood watching from the open door of the detached garage at the end of the drive, thirty feet away. One of her parents sat watching, as usual, from the bare branch above the nest of the tall white pine behind the garage.

Later I opened several lawn chairs, and we sat looking up. I thought, *this is our day so far—watching a bird. Nothing done. Nothing to show for our time.*

"It's a gift," you said as if answering my thoughts. "Being here, able to watch all this, is a blessing."

Every so often she would open her wings and flap them, trying to shake off the heavy wetness that soaked them, and her cries, those thin squeals, *eeeeeee, eeeeeee, eeeeeee,* which pierced the foggy, wet, and dimming afternoon, cut through the heavy air. In her drenched feathers, she seemed so much smaller and thinner now. Even her head looked no larger than a turkey's head.

When she stood still so her hanging wings, like a partly closed umbrella, took the beating from the large beads of rain that bounced hard as hail off her shoulders, you said, "Oh how I wish we could hold even a small covering over her dripping head."

I thought of Gogol's poor copy clerk, Akaky Akakievich, the worn overcoat, the Ukrainian cold in which he walked to work and home, and my heart ached.

If only she had known enough to glide down into one of the thick-branched spruce that lined the back of the house, but in this deluge, flying or gliding off the roof for her was out of the question. She would have to sit it out, now and again flapping and flapping her hanging wings, in the lightning and the thunder, and in the wind that swept rain across the roof and her cries across the universe.

## After the Rain

It was a cool and breezy morning after the rains, and the eaglet was sprawled out on Rose's cabin roof, this time on the west side in the sun, to dry her wings.

In the afternoon she was on the peak of our house again. You had seen her fly up off Rose's cabin roof and seen her circle and heard her thud and seen the landing with a wobble on the middle of the ridge of our roof, and you had called me out and phoned and invited the neighbors to come and see.

I ate something hurriedly and came out, but the eaglet was gone.

I sat for a long while on a bench on the deck at the back of the house that faced the lake. The cool breeze fluttered the highest leaves of the tall poplars. I thought it was a great day to soar, and then I saw one of the parents soaring, and I thought I saw an immature, our immature, on the right side of the parent, soaring, maybe a little clumsily, yet soaring, but in a blink this eaglet disappeared in the high, pale, lighted sky. I didn't see her again, only the parent, even when I squeezed my eyes closed before looking long and hard.

Thinking of the hot, hot days of early July and then the cool breeze of the morning after, the high winds of that afternoon, I may have been mistaken in my hopefulness, but I never heard the eaglet peeping in that afternoon.

This could have been the eaglet's flight day. I wanted her to find and get her wings. We all wanted her to. Ron, the neighbor, who had said the first year, especially the first winter, was the test of an immature eagle, maybe smiled and believed a little when I told him about my hopeful vision. It was that kind of day.

## Next Morning

Although adult eagles will sit on dead branches with their wings hung down to dry like a sweatshirt on a clothesline, next morning the eaglet was sprawled out again on Rose's cabin roof, trying to dry the night's dampness off her wings.

Later she was up on a branch twenty feet from the top of a tall poplar that was between our place and the place of the women next door. It was the first time we'd seen her so high. At one point the mother was alongside her, and the eaglet piped like a whiny child, but the mother didn't show any concern. Whining doesn't get an eaglet anywhere either, I guess. Then, the mother was gone.

At least up on a tall tree branch this young one seemed airborne, though later, when our firstborn came with his wife, the eaglet was in the middle of the gravel road at the top of our drive. In a while she went next door, to the women's place, and then came back to our place. We saw her halfway up the path from the lake, and I went behind her and with open arms tried to shepherd her into the woods. Instead, she continued up the path and hop-flew up our drive. I went inside.

When I heard her heavy step on the ridge of the roof again, I worried about her big feet, the large claws, damaging the shingles.

I went out and with a long wooden pole tried to coax her off the roof. She eyed my stick as I moved it side to side. Suddenly, as if feeling unwanted, she flew off downhill toward the lake. One of her breast feathers hung loose and downward, and she seemed unable to get enough lift, and like a plane losing altitude, her wings brushed and fluttered through the leaves and her belly scraped some branches of trees along the path to the lake and noisily skimmed the top of the oak at lakeside.

Confined closer to earth than any eagle we'd ever seen, this one spent her sixth day out in the world mostly grounded.

## Our Welcome Mat

When the eaglet was first out of the nest that Saturday morning in early July and we'd come back from judging the Seeley poetry slam at the Mooselips and from attending church, we had a message from the women next door about a hurt baby eagle in their yard.

The afternoon had been so hot and humid that the rain had come hard. You could understand their worry at seeing a baby eagle in their yard after a storm.

They were relieved to hear what we knew, that this was the bird's first day out of the nest. Not a hurt eaglet at all. They said their dogs had kept up a barrage of barking, though they were fenced in. "The barking," they said, "didn't seem to faze that bird."

"She's trying to fit in among us," I said, "if we can take her as she is."

But three days later when the eaglet was on the canvas cover of their pontoon, I saw one of them, Dawn, go down to the lake, and I heard her *shoo* and *shoo* that bird away. And you couldn't blame her. I had worried as much about my roof ridge shingles and used a stick pole to move the bird. Now I hoped that eaglet would fly sooner than later.

If she'd left the nest too soon, before her wings were fully grown, it wasn't our fault. If she was making herself a nuisance, she had to learn where it was okay to roost and where not. Besides, she was in mortal danger hanging around on the ground. For such a huge bird, being grounded, this bald eagle was just a sitting duck.

## So

So maybe after some pointed suggestion she flew off our roof, as after "shoos" she flew off the neighbor's pontoon cover.

Later we saw the eaglet atop the rotting birch trunk on the end of our point which is alongside the river channel to Birch Lake, and we heard her pining and pining, even when motor boats passed near.

Watching her fly, we could see how she got some altitude but not enough to give her the lift she needed to catch the winds and soar up where her parents were. Her landings, too, were still hard, off-center, and wobbly.

She was stuck mostly among us, and we'd lost interest. Our aspirations and our symbols look great from afar. Up close, we see some tarnish and glimpses of old flaws. We needed her to soar and soon, if she was to pull us away from ourselves and restore some mystery to herself.

### Enormous Wings

"... no longer an annoyance in her life but
an imaginary dot on the horizon of the sea."
—Gabriel Garcia Marquez,
*A Very Old Man with Enormous Wings*

Nine days out of the nest, and still the wing feathers weren't as long as she needed. The eaglet could fly over the lake but never high enough, and we wanted her to soar. We all needed her to be out of reach.

That day as we swam out and halfway across the lake, I saw her come over us and rise enough to land atop a dead poplar in front of the cabin of the women next door. They and their friends had their boats and dogs and water noodles out on the lake and didn't seem to notice or pay any attention to what the eaglet had accomplished.

## Aspirations & Symbols

The immature eagle is a better flyer now and less wobbly making a landing, though she still sits on Norb's white, lakeshore martin house. She's been staying close to the ground among us for over a month—too long, maybe. What with so much whiny peeping, dawn to dusk and at times after dark, there are days when even if we can still imagine her soaring, you can understand if we get to feeling sorry for ourselves and get tired of the constant noise and wish that bird elsewhere.

But then, there are those days when we don't hear her and we worry for her and dearly miss her and go out in a boat on the lake, twice and three times, looking for her.

## Nine Days Out

A ruckus of caws haunted the morning from the Birch Lake side of Rose's place. You had to figure the eaglet was close to where the crows were. It was good that she hung out near the water now. She had to learn to fish. It was her next big step. I remembered coaxing our firstborn with that "Yellow Ducky" he loved to hold. "Come. Come on. Come to daddy!" I'd keep repeating from across the room, so he would take some steps.

Probably the eaglet wouldn't be fed as much now. She needed to trim down for flying, and hunger would force her to look for fish. Still, she was peeping and peeping which was like a whining. Yesterday, she was on a dead birch on the point across the channel. We were happy for her, seeing her that far.

We had heard that Norb, who lives across the lake from the dead birch point, hated that bird because she would sit and poop on the cover of his pontoon.

# From the Badlands

We were in the Badlands where sharpened spires and buttes rose around us and where the hard, dry soil between slabs of moldered rocks spread along both sides of the road and out. Swallow and blink, and you could be driving on a road on the moon except the air was dry and burning, too. That afternoon the car thermometer registered ninety-six degrees Fahrenheit.

There were tall weeds and grasses and flowers—prairie plants.

Yet, after a week, we were glad to come back to our own place where trees rose as high as buttes and clear water spread away from us on every side.

The eaglet was still hanging close. You could hear her whining—from Norb's or from somewhere else across the lake—and her peeping touched us. We'd been gone and come back knowing that the bald eagle is holy to the Lakota Sioux.

I got in our old rowboat and went out looking for the eaglet.

# The Immature Eagle

The eaglet has been out of the nest for almost a month and now is able to fly back up to the nest in that high pine, and she'll sit peeping and peeping in the place where food had come easily.

Dawn to long after dusk you can hear her whining for food and attention.

During the day, when a parent finally shows, it's a madhouse of sound, the parent whistling, *Hello!* The eaglet, *Peeping! Squealing* and *Peeping!* The fish gets dropped to the ground—of course—airlift-like, I imagine. Then there is a great commotion of flapping wings, like a sail luffing downward.

Survival is not painless now. The eaglet has come down to the ground and has to scramble through brush, looking.

## Early August

By early August the immature eagle was soaring over the lake but still peeping often, like a whiny child, and she hung close to the ground and around the nest area. One moment she would be sitting on the roof of Norb's swallow apartment complex that's on a steel pole lakeside, and the next minute you might see her on a branch of the nest tree. We've all heard that a young eagle doesn't go back to the nest after leaving. That fact must have arisen only because of an immature's inability to get enough lift to go back to the nest on those first days out in the world.

Of this one, we could say she had trouble leaving home. Even after it was obvious she had moved out, we wondered if she regretted her decision. We would often see her coming back to the nest area, hanging around, probably longing for the easy life she had known. And who could blame her? How many of us were out of school, married even, and still running home for a quick visit to do laundry and pick up and take back a few of *Mamma's* leftovers?

I know in early August this immature eagle was soaring, but she was hanging close to home. Suddenly, one morning we heard piping and a flurry of whistling. I went out and saw her land behind the shed that's halfway up the hill that climbs gradually from the lake. She seemed crazy-desperate, the way she went back and forth on the ground and took little hops with a flap of those huge wings, and she piped and piped.

She hopped-flew, then, to the roof ridge of that twelve-foot-high shed and walked the roof ridge back and forth and kept cocking her head to the sides to look down. In a while she was back on the ground rushing through ferns and brush, searching.

Finally, I saw a parent swoop over low and drop a silvery fish for her. When she found it, she ripped a hunk from it and gulped it, and I saw the rest of that silveryness flop away, as if alive, from her huge black bill. She cocked her head to one side then the other, searching and searching with each eye. You could tell eagles are not so eagle-eyed close up. Close-up they could do with a strong pair of reading glasses, like many of us.

So, while our eaglet hadn't learned to fish for herself and while the parents still provided sometimes, you could tell she wasn't getting enough to eat. She looked trimmer or thinner. We had to figure her hunger would soon push her to learn to fish.

## We Had Been Waiting Since Early July

Toward the end of August, as I rushed to seed a patch of thin lawn, the immature eagle flew over like a grown-up, at tree-level, 150 to 200 feet up. Her whistle wasn't whiny then. And this morning as I watered the dry yellow straw over the seeded patch, in a cool September wind, I heard a high-pitched whistle and saw that young eagle again.

Oh, she was soaring on the updrafts, now. Maybe she saw me looking up, too, for she whistled again and tilted her head and left eye downward. Maybe to say she knew this place.

## Driving Toward Solon Springs

A dead, bloated deer in the swale of the right shoulder of the road and an immature eagle. An immature alongside six adult bald eagles and one raven having a great feast in the mid-morning sun. The deer belly was open, the innards spread out on the grassy, leafy cloth of the roadside dip.

Maybe this wasn't our immature who left the nest in the white pine behind our garage in early July, but she could have been. Seeing this gathering gave us heart. It was enough. You had to figure our eaglet, too, would be finding her way.

## After Three Days of Rain: Early November

Then, heavy rain and thirty-five to forty mile-per-hour winds and water-sodden trees suddenly cracking and falling and shaking the ground where they thumped.

Pacing back and forth, we whispered a prayer and looked out on a world we hardly knew. And I remembered the immature eagle on the roof ridge her first July out in the world when the deluge came—how she opened and flapped and flapped her wings and hopped to one end of the ridge, turned, and hopped back, flapping her soaked wings to shed the heavy rains. Who could forget how she sometimes called out? That pleading scream.

## Time Change

Because of the tilt of the earth, already the sun's angle is from the south enough so the light climbs trees on the opposite shore, and the air cools toward a blue-purple, cool pink above, cold gray on the far edges below—a lonely time, this earlier shifting day to dark.

But the immature eagle has suddenly come to a leafless popple above me. When I shift in my lawn chair, she turns her head, and holds her left eye over me. It could be the Divine Eye watching over everything that has brought this young one back for a while.

Still fine days for early November, though we've worried about this one making her way. I am glad when she flies off, after a while, and away from the home nest tree.

### Give It Up

Patches of sparkles
lap toward this shore
and warm waves
of a hesitant sun on wind
sweeping across the lake—
hounding the pines
above and behind me
and the dry blades of grass.

Everything says, *It's November.*
*Give it up.*
*And the poem won't save you.*
*You're hobbling through,*
*besides, this time.*

*Give it up,*
*though fresh watercress*
*fringes this north edge of the lake*
*and dry grass tufts show green roots*
*and the one who fetches you*
*found three feathers,*
*one with splotches*
*as blue as a May morning sky.*

## Since Dawn, Fine Snow Piled Up

You could see wind gusts
lift clumps and layers of pressed snow
off pine branches and roof shingles,
and still you could find fine snow dust
sifted into hairline crevices
you never knew.

But after dark
when the winds grew furious,
the house felt like too small a boat,
too far from shore,
in a sea of wind.

Under those waves of wind,
when the house creaked and groaned,
a shivering grabbed me and pressed
the weight of the storm on me
and stooped my shoulders.

Even huddled in a blanket in a chair
I was only a thin shell of skin,
inside a thin shell of wood,
enfolded by a raging storm,
and without you, dear reader,
no stronger than a house of straw.

## Out of a Cast, December 14, 2010

Because I could,
in late afternoon
I shoveled a path
down to the lake
and cleared a small circle.

I set down the shovel
and stood in the circle,
stomped with one,
then both feet—as light
as the dragonfly that crawled

out of its shuck—
split up the back and stuck
to the lake-side trunk of a birch.
Damp and bent,
that dragonfly began to stretch.

# 3

# A Resurrection

# The Heron's Eye

It's how the great blue heron stands looking at you. At your approach, she'll turn her head, and you'll wonder if you put away the leftover sweet corn, the sloppy Joe. Gnats flit about and land on the dirty dinner dishes stacked along the sink, the overripe tomato slices and leaves of romaine in their wetness, on the table.

Maybe you'll surprise yourself and come back to find you did put everything away and clean up, and you'll think that the heron's look was not meant to turn you toward the failings of your day. Maybe if you steer your canoe away from her corner of the lake soon enough, she won't fly, and you can feel that mostly you do try.

# In the Fall of Her Second Year

The bald eaglet we'd heard squawking, then peeping, in early spring never showed itself.

Once we saw the pair chase off their two-year-old who'd come by in late spring and hovered over the great nest that afternoon as the sky dimmed.

We all know what a hunger can make us do, and a long, cold winter could have clouded the two-year-old's memory—that instigator. Who can't imagine the scene? Strange, featherless wings whapping at her huge, touchy bill, as she pecked and pecked down. She would have had to cut her visit short, after. Afterward, we saw the pair chase off the immature eagle in that dimming afternoon.

And who doesn't remember the stab—of stopping by the old place and finding one's space full of strange stuff?

Often now we see the old pair, hopeful as ever, hauling sticks to the great nest, whistling greetings to each other, both coming and going.

# Gunflint Lake: Sunset

> ". . . the truth is the light
> and light is the truth."
> —from Ralph Ellison's *The Invisible Man*

A fiery sun
made a path toward us
on the rippled water
and scattered pink shavings
over the rest.

Night was falling.
Our differences encircled
us and a chill air.

But the light. It gathered us
at the edge of the lake,
and we stood.
We were pilgrims of the light.

## The Sound of the Creek

Already dead leaves were caught in the spills.
A cold draft blew, and the sound of the creek was slippery.

Listening, you could easily let go,
and the sound would carry your thoughts in its airy bubbles.
Soon you'd forget what you were thinking.

That miniature sunflower on the edge
and leaning over the water—
the wind pushed it toward the sound and toward the bubbling
in the shaft of light slithering through the shadows of trees and
down the way.

## Wind Had Jammed Logs of Foam Along Shore

Now warblers pepper the reeds.
Twitters and flurries of birds coming

and going. What if we hadn't come
out? What if we'd missed these birds
and that clump of ferns,
a burning bush in the dark?

Tomorrow the color will have fallen away.
The ferns will be burnished forever,
the orange farther than September.

Dear friends who may be reading
or stopping to puzzle over these words,

may these specks of light keep you.
All around us the dark deepens.
But these tiny birds flutter off reeds,
and the reeds wave, then settle back.

## Light and the Bats

Sometimes orange and purple hold the underside of clouds,
and we'll paddle toward the changing light
or stop in the middle of the lake to look up.

Bats criss-crossing in front of us sweep the air over our heads,
making us welcome.
We'll prolong our visit, then, like old friends.

The sky dims.
A coolness settles around us
as day and its wares grow more distant.

Look again and the light is gone. A sky of deep blue,
growing dark, eats up the rest of the day and memories of it.
A blue song may come, but the light and the bats make the night easier.

## October 2, 2010—Fractured Fibula in a Leg Cast

This is the autumn
you didn't want to miss.
Everywhere,
armfuls of migrating birds.
You turn, and leaves have colored.
Waves of them flutter down.
Today, a northwest wind,
Twenty to twenty-five miles per hour,
but a sunny sixty degrees.
Hatched bugs swarm
in dusty beams of light.

How easy—no, lovely—
is the lift of a finger.
A blue-gray nuthatch
on the scaly bark of a Norway—
you hear it—hangs downward
along the side of the tree.

# The Jar

When the sun finally came up, she was waiting on a hump of water lily roots that broke the surface like a bunch of floating pineapples in that watery place. She stretched her neck out to the first sun in days, because her body had already slowed past remembering and hope.

She concentrated on a need to fill herself with heat and push back the cold that filled the pockets of her shell and crept into the very lining of her skin.

As long as the sun touched, this one would cling to that place—let the world pass on its run. She'd gather all she could now and for as long . . . So she let the sun fill her with reminders. She might be a jar someone would unstop years later or question from afar.

# Fall

*—for Ron*

You could feel the change.
That day the wind blew a fragrance of lake across,

and the bald eagle narrowed his high circles and dropped.
His claws bubbled the lake surface
like a handful of pebbles we'd tossed.
Then he went off.

It was that kind of year.

I felt like blessing the neighbor
who'd showed me a patch of wild cranberries
in a bog of a lake we'd passed a thousand times before.

## Love and the Promise

Those times when our love reaches outside this place of ferns and trees, I think, *How will we find each other again once out of our skin?* Will you think, *Let's go out for a walk?* Will I sense your thought and be there, ready?

In every gust of wind, now, pine needles drop. The roll of things in motion. Even the lake will turn over soon, fish moving deeper. The promise is to come back hand in hand and walk a new earth not unlike this place.

## Hawk Ridge: Duluth, Minnesota

We're looking for hawks,
but we're late.
The fall migration is over.
Early November. Sunny.
Wind from the southwest.
A few juncos feed
on cracked corn
someone broadcast
up the gravel path
to the observation deck.

Three hawks pass:
a speckled gray,
a rough-legged in light phase,
a dark red-tailed.
Earlier a bald eagle soared
out over Superior.

You sit facing east.
I face northwest,
my leg cast resting on a cold boulder.
We don't talk.
It's a quiet place.
We've grown old together.
You are here for me.
I am here for you.

## Hobbling Around the Yard With My Right Foot and Ankle in a Cast to the Knee, I Remember the Immature Eagle Trying to Fly

This deer stands in the drive,
looking toward the house
and remembering the decorative Indian corn
we put out after a snowy March.

Calm, sunny November days
and our memories make us gentle.

Now I'd like to feed this deer
out of my hand. I bet I could, too,
but so close to hunting season,
it would be a thoughtless gesture.

Last year a young deer with a limp
hung close. We'd see her and feel for her.

Then, she was gone.
Though deer are hardly scarce here,
still, today I suddenly miss her.

## On Second Thought

I would like to throw my crutches away
and sit with that eagle in the dead birch in the bay,
watching the mallards come in at dusk.

When he went down fast, skimming the lake
where the mallard had ducked under, maybe it was
already too dark, and he knew it. He came back
from across and over her, hardly dipping,
and she must have sensed her great luck
and held the last squawk fast in her throat,
like not voicing an afterthought,
willingly letting the dark have the last word.

How lovely the lift of a finger, the hand holding a pen.

## Last Light

    I gather
the last light—armfuls
for the one inside to hold.

    The strong wind
is gone. Brown pine needles
and curled leaves

        restless around us—
nut hatches,
deer shuffling through.

## My Coat

Today snow silted the ice-glaze rain left on the roads. The temperature is in the twenties, but wind chills to the bone. My fine coat. Its blue-black windbreak shell and gray fleece liner raise shivers of warmth even indoors if you think of the coat— like being inside a fishing shed whapped by wind.

What a revelation that a coat should give such comfort. As much as a squashed pillow gives you in the darkest night. Think of the solid footing a glass of water gives your distant body when you wake.

Still, our coats enfold much less for us than for Akaky in Gogol's story. After two thieves yanked off his coat and ran away with it, he never got it back and never warmed up again. He took to his deathbed.

# From Kabir

"as the river gives itself into the ocean,
what is inside me moves inside you."
—Kabir

Yesterday I was a man with a broken leg.
Then you filled me with light.

Today I am like the Brule
emptying itself into Superior.

All afternoon we smiled toward each other.
I saw the trees alive with insects and birds.

## Ice Caves Along the South Shore

Day and night the heave and pull had left ripples and ridges across the ice, and though the great lake was hidden from you and you walked with a lifetime of care, the moonscape look of the ice-crust lifted shivers on you.

Sometimes a faint rumble underfoot caught you mid-breath and made you swallow all reason.

Only the dark line of clouds along the horizon could lift an eyelid so the falling sun spread a momentary path of light toward your shore.

## February 8, 2010

Wind and light snow
whiten the air over the lake.
A few hours and tracks from our snowshoes fill and disappear,

but then we love how the lake
cleans up after us—that wind and its broom of snow.

Mid-afternoon in a hint of sun
the spruce flutter with birds—
chickadees and a few loud blue jays sweep winter off our thoughts.

## February 14, 2010

Mid-February, and the Christmas cactus has outdone itself in the south window. Floating flowers hover above the green like armfuls of hummingbirds. Here, there is no winter. Reds came—old friends, picking up conversations where we left off years before. And the tallest forked shoot at the back of the pot wouldn't sit still. In a couple days, it bloomed—two whitish-pink flowers.

After a while, you remembered how you'd salvaged that shoot from a plant your mother gave you years before. You'd missed her dying. It was all right.

## Early March, 2015

In the afternoon
snow had melted on the lake,
and there were blue puddles,
and in places the lake ice showed clear.
Trees were alive with flutters and twitters and chirps.
Air warmed and floated up to the sun,

and we stood looking up. It's a habit
where trees are thin and tall, searching for light.
Can you blame us if we were buoyant,
then, talking and talking,
standing on tip-toes, and felt airy
and as expectant as the lift of a wing.

## When April Was April—April, 2009

A thin plate of ice
hung to the shaded
edge of our lakeshore,
but robins were everywhere,
and earlier that morning
the one in Mike's scrapyard,
stood head high, feathers
preened—poised and perky.

# May, 2015

i.

Saturday, April 26, six days
before the five-day stay in St. Mary's hospital, Duluth,
we were on the way home from St. John's, Minnesota,
where we'd missed Father Don's
acceptance speech for his citation and medal.
That Saturday on the way home
she said, "This is it. I'm changing my life.
I'm starting anew.
I'm going to be a new person.
Eating. Eating,
and pretending it doesn't matter.
Mindless eating . . .
I'm going to be pretty,
the size I was when we were married.
I can do it.
No more cappuccinos.
Sweet creamers with coffee.
I'm cutting sugar.
Caffeine.
We'll do colorful foods.
Surround ourselves with all beautiful things.
I'll surround myself with serious music—
Mozart, Bach, Wagner.
I love Wagner's *Siegfried*!" She said,
"I could listen to Wagner's *Siegfried Idyll* all day."

She was on a roll.
I didn't question any of her music choices.
I didn't say anything,
not even the thought
that even a recommitted person
could only endure the same CD so long.
Was she also recommitting herself
to the virtue of patience?
I didn't say anything.
I drove. I listened and drove.

"And Copeland," she said.
"You can't forget Copeland.
Every day I could do Copeland.
I never get tired of listening to Copeland."

She said, "I'm changing my life.
I haven't felt like eating,
and I'm not going back.
Not ever!"

That previous Monday night in April
when the Pittsburg Symphony played for us,
she'd felt a pain
from her lower right side cut across her belly.

Later, two weeks later,
when I asked her in the hospital, she said,
"Worse than any pain I had while giving birth.
Much . . . much more painful." She said,
"It went away.
I thought—a stomachache,
like those I often get.

Something I ate, I thought.
After a while it went away,
and I forgot.
The music was so . . . was so . . .
I love Dvorak. I love Tchaikovsky.
The harp . . . the oboe . . .
It was all *soooooo* beautiful."

"If you had told me," I said.

"I didn't want to ruin the concert," she said.

She only threw up later,
after the concert,
and most next day.

## ii.

That April Tuesday we left Pennsylvania at 5:00 a.m.
She was sick across wide Ohio,
across Indiana, and up Illinois.
We finally stopped in Tomah, Wisconsin,
after 8:00 p.m. central time,
fifteen-plus hours later,
only four hours from home.
It was snowing,
a mix of rain and snow sticking to the roads.
Motels along the interstate
had filled up early.
In the Best Western, she was sick.
Threw up again next morning.

We made the Essentia Health Clinic, Hayward,
before 1:00 p.m. on Wednesday,
where she was checked for the bad flu she said she had.

Friday of that end of April
we were dressed up and in the old gym of St. John's.
The meal was a filet mignon,
a pound chunk, at least, per plate.
Somehow, I'd missed the vegetarian entrée box.
I ate the salad, the fingerling potatoes,
mine and all but two of hers,
a warm bun (no butter),
and the pretty, key-lime cheesecake ball.
She had one bite of hers, to taste it,
the two smallest potatoes, a leaf or two of salad,
a hunk of buttered bun,
and a few swallows of the Propel water that she carried.
(At the clinic the NP had instructed her to drink
Propel or Gatorade.) She took a few more
sips as we waited for the program to begin.

iii.

"Here is Father Don," I said.
She looked up.
There was a shuffling.
The cellist, artist-in-residence from New York,
who had stayed over for the celebration
and had left us struck, left the stage.
The college president got up again,
and Father Don sat down.


"There," I said, "Father Don is getting up."
"Finally," she said.
"We made it. You made it," I said.
"Your first meal since Tuesday morning.
This is your resurrection.
Father Don is walking up to the podium."

"They all went on so long.
Why did they have to go on for so long?"
she said. "I hope I make it."

"You can," I said.

"I hope I can."

"You can."

"I don't think I can," she said.
"They went on too long."

iv.

I led us out
along the dark-draped north wall of the old gym
and for an instant shouldered all their eyes.

"Let's get some air," I said,
after the bathroom stop.

Outside,
it was misting.
The wind blew cold.
I turned to try the door.
It had locked behind us.
We'd left our coats
in our friend Mary's car.

In the student commons
she headed for the bathroom
and took so long . . .
I paced.

In the Tomah Best Western,
the past Wednesday morning,
in the shower,
she'd passed out.
I'd heard the thump.
After that,
when she entered a bathroom,
I always waited
gun shy.

Now,
I heard her retching.
Another woman came,
entered the bathroom
and came out soon
and rushed for the outside doors.
I decided not to ask
anything of her.
Then I heard
the retching again.

v.

Twelve days
after that Monday night
when the Pittsburg Symphony played Dvorak and Tchaikovsky,
sweet music she would always remember with the pain,
she came home
from a "Keep the Eau Claire Lakes Clean" luncheon,
having eaten a quarter-sandwich of ham, tomato, and lettuce
and got into bed.
She was exhausted. Freezing.
Her temperature was 101.7°.
At 9:00 p.m. that Friday night
we were in ER, in St. Mary's Hospital, Duluth, Minnesota.

The rest is a story
of CAT scans
and IVs,
of a ruptured appendix
and a procedure
and a drain bottle for five weeks
to empty the fistula—
the gift her body made around the poison
and saved her life.
It's a story of potent antibiotics
and constant nausea,
of poor sleep nights
and night sweats,
and a loss of weight—
eighteen to twenty pounds.
It is a story in which the taste
for food and drink,
even water,
is a distant memory—hardly alive.

vi.

But that Saturday
when we were on our way home
after we'd missed Father Don's acceptance
speech for the SJU's President's citation and medal
and she suddenly stated her revelation
that she was changing her life,
nothing had yet been resolved.
It would be another week before her diagnosis
and procedure.

## vii.

"Today I'm here," she said
that morning in May.
It was forty-five degrees, sunny, blue sky,
trees leafing out,
and we were doing
our morning's three miles.
The check-up in a week
would initially clear her.
The drain would probably finally come out.
There were roses in her cheeks.
Her eyes and her words were there.
She was beside me,
and she was keeping up.

## Waiting

The red fox waiting for us to drive past
had a mouthful. Maybe a char-grilled rib
that she held her head up to show—
you've imagined a taste for so long,
your mouth sits in awe.
                                    Warm saliva
oozes around your tongue, but you wait.

You could be on the way to meet the one
who sometimes makes you forget to breathe.

## Acknowledgements

The author wishes to thank the editors of the following publications in which some of his poems first appeared: *Commonweal*, *Letters Not Sent* (a handmade, limited edition book by Susan Pagnucci, Robinson Lake Imprints), and *Whistling Shade*.